Printed and bound in Great Britain by Lulu Press, Inc.

Published in London in December 2018

Copyright © 2018 by Jakub Tencl, Ph.D

ISBN: 978-0-244-44056-5

www.ihypnosis.org.uk

My Plan For Fulfilling of My Life Dreams

What would I like to do?

1.
2.
3.
4.

Who is involved in my idea what to do?

1.
2.
3.
4.

What are my expectations?

1.
2.
3.
4.

Is that idea one of my life dreams?

1	☐ Yes	☐ No
2	☐ Yes	☐ No
3	☐ Yes	☐ No
4	☐ Yes	☐ No

Am I Felling *Stress?*

How intense is my stress on the scale from 1 to 20 (Most intense)	
Monday	
Tuesday	
Wednesday	
Thursday	
Friday	

Do I need to take a break?		
Monday	Yes	No
Tuesday	Yes	No
Wednesday	Yes	No
Thursday	Yes	No
Friday	Yes	No

If no, finishing your activity doesn't mean that you can relax, true?		
Monday	Yes	No
Tuesday	Yes	No
Wednesday	Yes	No
Thursday	Yes	No
Friday	Yes	No

Am I happy at this moment		
Monday	Yes	No
Tuesday	Yes	No
Wednesday	Yes	No
Thursday	Yes	No
Friday	Yes	No

If no, why is important to continue in my activity?		
Monday	Yes	No
Tuesday	Yes	No
Wednesday	Yes	No
Thursday	Yes	No
Friday	Yes	No

If no, do I want to be happy?		
Monday	Yes	No
Tuesday	Yes	No
Wednesday	Yes	No
Thursday	Yes	No
Friday	Yes	No

My Plan to Enjoy My Day

Today's day and date: [M] [T] [W] [T] [F] [S] [S] Day: [   ] Month: [   ] Year: [   ]

What did you enjoy most today?

Assign intensity on the scale from 1 to 20 (most intense)

>>Stress : _____

>>Overall Mood : _____

What are you grateful for today?

>>Tiredness : _____

>>Length of Sleeping (In hours) : _____

What would you like to do for yourself?
1. _____
2. _____
3. _____
4. _____

The present moment is filled with joy and happiness. If you are attentive, you will see it.
— Thich Nhat Hanh

My rewards for what has been successfully Done or just for the enjoyment of the day

My priorities for today
1. _____
2. _____
3. _____
4. _____

What inspired you today?

Did you have 5 minutes of stillness this morning?

[ ] Yes   [ ] No

Did you realize a tense feeling during the day and after the experience of stillness this morning

[ ] Yes   [ ] No

[ ] Morning Routine   [ ] Evening Routine

My Plan to Enjoy My Day

Today's day and date: [M] [T] [W] [T] [F] [S] [S]   Day: [   ]   Month: [   ]   Year: [   ]

What did you enjoy most today?

Assign intensity on the scale from 1 to 20 (most intense)

>>Stress :

>>Overall Mood :

What are you grateful for today?

>>Tiredness :

>>Length of Sleeping (In hours) :

What would you like to do for yourself?
1.
2.
3.
4.

The present moment is filled with joy and happiness. If you are attentive, you will see it.
Thich Nhat Hanh

My rewards for what has been successfully Done or just for the enjoyment of the day

My priorities for today
1.
2.
3.
4.

What inspired you today?

Did you have 5 minutes of stillness this morning?

[ ] Yes   [ ] No

Did you realize a tense feeling during the day and after the experience of stillness this morning

[ ] Yes   [ ] No

[ ] Morning Routine   [ ] Evening Routine

My Plan to Enjoy My Day

Today's day and date: [M] [T] [W] [T] [F] [S] [S]　Day: [　　]　Month: [　　]　Year: [　　]

What did you enjoy most today?

What are you grateful for today?

Assign intensity on the scale from 1 to 20 (most intense)

>>Stress :

>>Overall Mood :

>>Tiredness :

>>Length of Sleeping (In hours) :

What would you like to do for yourself?
1. _____
2. _____
3. _____
4. _____

The present moment is filled with joy and happiness. If you are attentive, you will see it.
— Thich Nhat Hanh

My rewards for what has been successfully Done or just for the enjoyment of the day

My priorities for today
1. _____
2. _____
3. _____
4. _____

What inspired you today?

Did you have 5 minutes of stillness this morning?

☐ Yes　　☐ No

Did you realize a tense feeling during the day and after the experience of stillness this morning

☐ Yes　　☐ No

☐ Morning Routine　☐ Evening Routine

My Plan to Enjoy My Day

Today's day and date: [M] [T] [W] [T] [F] [S] [S] Day: [   ] Month: [   ] Year: [   ]

What did you enjoy most today?

Assign intensity on the scale from 1 to 20 (most intense)

>>Stress :

>>Overall Mood :

What are you grateful for today?

>>Tiredness :

>>Length of Sleeping (In hours) :

What would you like to do for yourself?
1.
2.
3.
4.

The present moment is filled with joy and happiness. If you are attentive, you will see it.
— Thich Nhat Hanh

My rewards for what has been successfully Done or just for the enjoyment of the day

My priorities for today
1.
2.
3.
4.

What inspired you today?

Did you have 5 minutes of stillness this morning?

[ ] Yes   [ ] No

Did you realize a tense feeling during the day and after the experience of stillness this morning

[ ] Yes   [ ] No

[ ] Morning Routine [ ] Evening Routine

My Plan to Enjoy My Day

Today's day and date: [M] [T] [W] [T] [F] [S] [S] Day: [   ] Month: [   ] Year: [   ]

What did you enjoy most today?

Assign intensity on the scale from 1 to 20 (most intense)

>>Stress :

>>Overall Mood :

>>Tiredness :

>>Length of Sleeping (In hours) :

What are you grateful for today?

What would you like to do for yourself?
1.
2.
3.
4.

The present moment is filled with joy and happiness. If you are attentive, you will see it.
— Thich Nhat Hanh

My rewards for what has been successfully Done or just for the enjoyment of the day

My priorities for today
1.
2.
3.
4.

What inspired you today?

Did you have 5 minutes of stillness this morning?

[ ] Yes   [ ] No

Did you realize a tense feeling during the day and after the experience of stillness this morning

[ ] Yes   [ ] No

[ ] Morning Routine [ ] Evening Routine

My Plan to Enjoy My Day

Today's day and date: [M] [T] [W] [T] [F] [S] [S]   Day: [   ]   Month: [   ]   Year: [   ]

What did you enjoy most today?

Assign intensity on the scale from 1 to 20 (most intense)

>>Stress :

>>Overall Mood :

What are you grateful for today?

>>Tiredness :

>>Length of Sleeping (In hours) :

What would you like to do for yourself?
1.
2.
3.
4.

The present moment is filled with joy and happiness. If you are attentive, you will see it.

— Thich Nhat Hanh

My rewards for what has been successfully Done or just for the enjoyment of the day

My priorities for today
1.
2.
3.
4.

What inspired you today?

Did you have 5 minutes of stillness this morning?

[ ] Yes   [ ] No

Did you realize a tense feeling during the day and after the experience of stillness this morning

[ ] Yes   [ ] No

[ ] Morning Routine   [ ] Evening Routine

My Plan to Enjoy My Day

Today's day and date: [M] [T] [W] [T] [F] [S] [S]   Day: [　　]   Month: [　　]   Year: [　　]

What did you enjoy most today?

Assign intensity on the scale from 1 to 20 (most intense)

>>Stress :

>>Overall Mood :

What are you grateful for today?

>>Tiredness :

>>Length of Sleeping (In hours) :

What would you like to do for yourself?

1.
2.
3.
4.

> The present moment is filled with joy and happiness. If you are attentive, you will see it.
> Thich Nhat Hanh

My rewards for what has been successfully Done or just for the enjoyment of the day

My priorities for today

1.
2.
3.
4.

What inspired you today?

Did you have 5 minutes of stillness this morning?

☐ Yes   ☐ No

Did you realize a tense feeling during the day and after the experience of stillness this morning

☐ Yes   ☐ No

☐ Morning Routine ☐ Evening Routine

My Plan For Fulfilling of My Life Dreams

What would I like to do?

1	
2	
3	
4	

Who is involved in my idea what to do?

1	
2	
3	
4	

What are my expectations?

1	
2	
3	
4	

Is that idea one of my life dreams?

1	☐ Yes	☐ No
2	☐ Yes	☐ No
3	☐ Yes	☐ No
4	☐ Yes	☐ No

Am I Felling Stress?

How intense is my stress on the scale from 1 to 20 (Most intense)	
Monday	
Tuesday	
Wednesday	
Thursday	
Friday	

Do I need to take a break?		
Monday	Yes	No
Tuesday	Yes	No
Wednesday	Yes	No
Thursday	Yes	No
Friday	Yes	No

If no, finishing your activity doesn't mean that you can relax, true?		
Monday	Yes	No
Tuesday	Yes	No
Wednesday	Yes	No
Thursday	Yes	No
Friday	Yes	No

Am I happy at this moment		
Monday	Yes	No
Tuesday	Yes	No
Wednesday	Yes	No
Thursday	Yes	No
Friday	Yes	No

If no, why is important to continue in my activity?		
Monday	Yes	No
Tuesday	Yes	No
Wednesday	Yes	No
Thursday	Yes	No
Friday	Yes	No

If no, do I want to be happy?		
Monday	Yes	No
Tuesday	Yes	No
Wednesday	Yes	No
Thursday	Yes	No
Friday	Yes	No

My Plan to ~~Enjoy~~ My Day

Today's day and date: [M] [T] [W] [T] [F] [S] [S]   Day: [   ]   Month: [   ]   Year: [   ]

What did you enjoy most today?

Assign intensity on the scale from 1 to 20 (most intense)

>>Stress :

>>Overall Mood :

What are you grateful for today?

>>Tiredness :

>>Length of Sleeping (In hours) :

What would you like to do for yourself?
1. _____
2. _____
3. _____
4. _____

The present moment is filled with joy and happiness. If you are attentive, you will see it.
— *Thich Nhat Hanh*

My rewards for what has been successfully Done or just for the enjoyment of the day

My priorities for today
1. _____
2. _____
3. _____
4. _____

What inspired you today?

Did you have 5 minutes of stillness this morning?

☐ Yes   ☐ No

Did you realize a tense feeling during the day and after the experience of stillness this morning

☐ Yes   ☐ No

☐ Morning Routine   ☐ Evening Routine

My Plan to Enjoy My Day

Today's day and date: [M] [T] [W] [T] [F] [S] [S]   Day: [   ]   Month: [   ]   Year: [   ]

What did you enjoy most today?

Assign intensity on the scale from 1 to 20 (most intense)

>>Stress :

>>Overall Mood :

What are you grateful for today?

>>Tiredness :

>>Length of Sleeping (In hours) :

What would you like to do for yourself?
1.
2.
3.
4.

The present moment is filled with joy and happiness. If you are attentive, you will see it.
— Thich Nhat Hanh

My rewards for what has been successfully Done or just for the enjoyment of the day

My priorities for today
1.
2.
3.
4.

What inspired you today?

Did you have 5 minutes of stillness this morning?

☐ Yes   ☐ No

Did you realize a tense feeling during the day and after the experience of stillness this morning

☐ Yes   ☐ No

☐ Morning Routine   ☐ Evening Routine

My Plan to Enjoy My Day

Today's day and date: [M] [T] [W] [T] [F] [S] [S] Day: [ ] Month: [ ] Year: [ ]

What did you enjoy most today?

Assign intensity on the scale from 1 to 20 (most intense)

>>Stress :

>>Overall Mood :

What are you grateful for today?

>>Tiredness :

>>Length of Sleeping (In hours) :

What would you like to do for yourself?
1.
2.
3.
4.

The present moment is filled with joy and happiness. If you are attentive, you will see it.

Thich Nhat Hanh

My rewards for what has been successfully Done or just for the enjoyment of the day

My priorities for today
1.
2.
3.
4.

What inspired you today?

Did you have 5 minutes of stillness this morning?

[ ] Yes   [ ] No

Did you realize a tense feeling during the day and after the experience of stillness this morning

[ ] Yes   [ ] No

[ ] Morning Routine [ ] Evening Routine

My Plan to Enjoy My Day

Today's day and date: [M] [T] [W] [T] [F] [S] [S]   Day: [   ]   Month: [   ]   Year: [   ]

What did you enjoy most today?

Assign intensity on the scale from 1 to 20 (most intense)

>>Stress :

>>Overall Mood :

What are you grateful for today?

>>Tiredness :

>>Length of Sleeping (In hours) :

What would you like to do for yourself?
1.
2.
3.
4.

The present moment is filled with joy and happiness. If you are attentive, you will see it.
Thich Nhat Hanh

My rewards for what has been successfully Done or just for the enjoyment of the day

My priorities for today
1.
2.
3.
4.

What inspired you today?

Did you have 5 minutes of stillness this morning?

[ ] Yes   [ ] No

Did you realize a tense feeling during the day and after the experience of stillness this morning

[ ] Yes   [ ] No

[ ] Morning Routine   [ ] Evening Routine

My Plan to Enjoy My Day

Today's day and date: [M] [T] [W] [T] [F] [S] [S]   Day: [ ]   Month: [ ]   Year: [ ]

What did you enjoy most today?

Assign intensity on the scale from 1 to 20 (most intense)

>>Stress :

>>Overall Mood :

What are you grateful for today?

>>Tiredness :

>>Length of Sleeping (In hours) :

What would you like to do for yourself?
1.
2.
3.
4.

The present moment is filled with joy and happiness. If you are attentive, you will see it.
— Thich Nhat Hanh

My rewards for what has been successfully Done or just for the enjoyment of the day

My priorities for today
1.
2.
3.
4.

What inspired you today?

Did you have 5 minutes of stillness this morning?

[ ] Yes   [ ] No

Did you realize a tense feeling during the day and after the experience of stillness this morning

[ ] Yes   [ ] No

[ ] Morning Routine   [ ] Evening Routine

My Plan to ~~Enjoy~~ My Day

Today's day and date: [M] [T] [W] [T] [F] [S] [S]   Day: [   ]   Month: [   ]   Year: [   ]

What did you enjoy most today?

Assign intensity on the scale from 1 to 20 (most intense)

>>Stress :

>>Overall Mood :

What are you grateful for today?

>>Tiredness :

>>Length of Sleeping (In hours) :

What would you like to do for yourself?
1. _____
2. _____
3. _____
4. _____

The present moment is filled with joy and happiness. If you are attentive, you will see it.
— Thich Nhat Hanh

My rewards for what has been successfully Done or just for the enjoyment of the day

My priorities for today
1. _____
2. _____
3. _____
4. _____

What inspired you today?

Did you have 5 minutes of stillness this morning?

☐ Yes   ☐ No

Did you realize a tense feeling during the day and after the experience of stillness this morning

☐ Yes   ☐ No

☐ Morning Routine   ☐ Evening Routine

My Plan to Enjoy My Day

Today's day and date: [M] [T] [W] [T] [F] [S] [S] Day: [   ] Month: [   ] Year: [   ]

What did you enjoy most today?

Assign intensity on the scale from 1 to 20 (most intense)

>>Stress :

>>Overall Mood :

What are you grateful for today?

>>Tiredness :

>>Length of Sleeping (In hours) :

What would you like to do for yourself?
1.
2.
3.
4.

The present moment is filled with joy and happiness. If you are attentive, you will see it.
Thich Nhat Hanh

My rewards for what has been successfully Done or just for the enjoyment of the day

My priorities for today
1.
2.
3.
4.

What inspired you today?

Did you have 5 minutes of stillness this morning?

☐ Yes   ☐ No

Did you realize a tense feeling during the day and after the experience of stillness this morning

☐ Yes   ☐ No

☐ Morning Routine   ☐ Evening Routine

My Plan For Fulfilling of My Life Dreams

What would I like to do?

1.
2.
3.
4.

Who is involved in my idea what to do?

1.
2.
3.
4.

What are my expectations?

1.
2.
3.
4.

Is that idea one of my life dreams?

1. ☐ Yes   ☐ No
2. ☐ Yes   ☐ No
3. ☐ Yes   ☐ No
4. ☐ Yes   ☐ No

Am I Felling Stress?

How intense is my stress on the scale from 1 to 20 (Most intense)	
Monday	
Tuesday	
Wednesday	
Thursday	
Friday	

Do I need to take a break?		
Monday	Yes	No
Tuesday	Yes	No
Wednesday	Yes	No
Thursday	Yes	No
Friday	Yes	No

If no, finishing your activity doesn't mean that you can relax, true?		
Monday	Yes	No
Tuesday	Yes	No
Wednesday	Yes	No
Thursday	Yes	No
Friday	Yes	No

Am I happy at this moment		
Monday	Yes	No
Tuesday	Yes	No
Wednesday	Yes	No
Thursday	Yes	No
Friday	Yes	No

If no, why is important to continue in my activity?		
Monday	Yes	No
Tuesday	Yes	No
Wednesday	Yes	No
Thursday	Yes	No
Friday	Yes	No

If no, do I want to be happy?		
Monday	Yes	No
Tuesday	Yes	No
Wednesday	Yes	No
Thursday	Yes	No
Friday	Yes	No

My Plan to Enjoy My Day

Today's day and date: [M] [T] [W] [T] [F] [S] [S]   Day: [ ]   Month: [ ]   Year: [ ]

What did you enjoy most today?

Assign intensity on the scale from 1 to 20 (most intense)

>>Stress :

>>Overall Mood :

What are you grateful for today?

>>Tiredness :

>>Length of Sleeping (In hours) :

What would you like to do for yourself?
1.
2.
3.
4.

The present moment is filled with joy and happiness. If you are attentive, you will see it.
Thich Nhat Hanh

My rewards for what has been successfully Done or just for the enjoyment of the day

My priorities for today
1.
2.
3.
4.

What inspired you today?

Did you have 5 minutes of stillness this morning?

☐ Yes   ☐ No

Did you realize a tense feeling during the day and after the experience of stillness this morning

☐ Yes   ☐ No

☐ Morning Routine ☐ Evening Routine

My Plan to Enjoy My Day

Today's day and date: [M] [T] [W] [T] [F] [S] [S]   Day: [   ]   Month: [   ]   Year: [   ]

What did you enjoy most today?

Assign intensive on the scale from 1 to 20 (most intense)

>>Stress :

>>Overall Mood :

What are you grateful for today?

>>Tiredness :

>>Length of Sleeping (In hours) :

What would you like to do for yourself?
1.
2.
3.
4.

The present moment is filled with joy and happiness. If you are attentive, you will see it.
Thich Nhat Hanh

My rewards for what has been successfully Done or just for the enjoyment of the day

My priorities for today
1.
2.
3.
4.

What inspired you today?

Did you have 5 minutes of stillness this morning?

[ ] Yes   [ ] No

Did you realize a tense feeling during the day and after the experience of stillness this morning

[ ] Yes   [ ] No

[ ] Morning Routine   [ ] Evening Routine

My Plan to Enjoy My Day

Today's day and date: | M | T | W | T | F | S | S | Day: [   ]   Month: [   ]   Year: [   ]

What did you enjoy most today?

Assign intensity on the scale from 1 to 20 (most intense)

>>Stress :

>>Overall Mood :

>>Tiredness :

What are you grateful for today?

>>Length of Sleeping (In hours) :

What would you like to do for yourself?
1.
2.
3.
4.

The present moment is filled with joy and happiness. If you are attentive, you will see it.
— Thich Nhat Hanh

My rewards for what has been successfully Done or just for the enjoyment of the day

My priorities for today
1.
2.
3.
4.

What inspired you today?

Did you have 5 minutes of stillness this morning?

☐ Yes   ☐ No

Did you realize a tense feeling during the day and after the experience of stillness this morning

☐ Yes   ☐ No

☐ Morning Routine   ☐ Evening Routine

My Plan to Enjoy My Day

Today's day and date: | M | T | W | T | F | S | S | Day: [   ]   Month: [   ]   Year: [   ]

What did you enjoy most today?

Assign intensity on the scale from 1 to 20 (most intense)

>>Stress :

>>Overall Mood :

What are you grateful for today?

>>Tiredness :

>>Length of Sleeping (In hours) :

What would you like to do for yourself?
1.
2.
3.
4.

The present moment is filled with joy and happiness. If you are attentive, you will see it.
— Thich Nhat Hanh

My rewards for what has been successfully Done or just for the enjoyment of the day

My priorities for today
1.
2.
3.
4.

What inspired you today?

Did you have 5 minutes of stillness this morning?

☐ Yes   ☐ No

Did you realize a tense feeling during the day and after the experience of stillness this morning

☐ Yes   ☐ No

☐ Morning Routine   ☐ Evening Routine

My Plan to Enjoy My Day

Today's day and date: [M] [T] [W] [T] [F] [S] [S] Day: [ ] Month: [ ] Year: [ ]

What did you enjoy most today?

Assign intensity on the scale from 1 to 20 (most intense)

>>Stress :

>>Overall Mood :

What are you grateful for today?

>>Tiredness :

>>Length of Sleeping (In hours) :

What would you like to do for yourself?
1.
2.
3.
4.

The present moment is filled with joy and happiness. If you are attentive, you will see it.
Thich Nhat Hanh

My rewards for what has been successfully Done or just for the enjoyment of the day

My priorities for today
1.
2.
3.
4.

What inspired you today?

Did you have 5 minutes of stillness this morning?

[ ] Yes   [ ] No

Did you realize a tense feeling during the day and after the experience of stillness this morning

[ ] Yes   [ ] No

[ ] Morning Routine   [ ] Evening Routine

My Plan to Enjoy My Day

Today's day and date: [M] [T] [W] [T] [F] [S] [S]　Day: [　　]　Month: [　　]　Year: [　　]

What did you enjoy most today?

Assign intensity on the scale from 1 to 20 (most intense)

>>Stress :

>>Overall Mood :

>>Tiredness :

What are you grateful for today?

>>Length of Sleeping (In hours) :

What would you like to do for yourself?
1.
2.
3.
4.

The present moment is filled with joy and happiness. If you are attentive, you will see it.

Thich Nhat Hanh

My rewards for what has been successfully Done or just for the enjoyment of the day

My priorities for today
1.
2.
3.
4.

What inspired you today?

Did you have 5 minutes of stillness this morning?

[ ] Yes　　[ ] No

Did you realize a tense feeling during the day and after the experience of stillness this morning

[ ] Yes　　[ ] No

[ ] Morning Routine　[ ] Evening Routine

My Plan to Enjoy My Day

Today's day and date: [M] [T] [W] [T] [F] [S] [S]   Day: [   ]   Month: [   ]   Year: [   ]

What did you enjoy most today?

Assign intensity on the scale from 1 to 20 (most intense)

>>Stress :

>>Overall Mood :

>>Tiredness :

What are you grateful for today?

>>Length of Sleeping (In hours) :

What would you like to do for yourself?
1.
2.
3.
4.

The present moment is filled with joy and happiness. If you are attentive, you will see it.
— Thich Nhat Hanh

My rewards for what has been successfully Done or just for the enjoyment of the day

My priorities for today
1.
2.
3.
4.

What inspired you today?

Did you have 5 minutes of stillness this morning?

☐ Yes   ☐ No

Did you realize a tense feeling during the day and after the experience of stillness this morning

☐ Yes   ☐ No

☐ Morning Routine   ☐ Evening Routine

My Plan For Fulfilling of My Life Dreams

What would I like to do?

1	
2	
3	
4	

Who is involved in my idea what to do?

1	
2	
3	
4	

What are my expectations?

1	
2	
3	
4	

Is that idea one of my life dreams?

1	☐ Yes	☐ No
2	☐ Yes	☐ No
3	☐ Yes	☐ No
4	☐ Yes	☐ No

Am I Felling Stress?

How intense is my stress on the scale from 1 to 20 (Most intense)	
Monday	
Tuesday	
Wednesday	
Thursday	
Friday	

Do I need to take a break?		
Monday	Yes	No
Tuesday	Yes	No
Wednesday	Yes	No
Thursday	Yes	No
Friday	Yes	No

If no, finishing your activity doesn't mean that you can relax, true?		
Monday	Yes	No
Tuesday	Yes	No
Wednesday	Yes	No
Thursday	Yes	No
Friday	Yes	No

Am I happy at this moment		
Monday	Yes	No
Tuesday	Yes	No
Wednesday	Yes	No
Thursday	Yes	No
Friday	Yes	No

If no, why is important to continue in my activity?		
Monday	Yes	No
Tuesday	Yes	No
Wednesday	Yes	No
Thursday	Yes	No
Friday	Yes	No

If no, do I want to be happy?		
Monday	Yes	No
Tuesday	Yes	No
Wednesday	Yes	No
Thursday	Yes	No
Friday	Yes	No

My Plan to Enjoy My Day

Today's day and date: | M | T | W | T | F | S | S | Day: [   ]   Month: [   ]   Year: [   ]

What did you enjoy most today?

Assign intensity on the scale from 1 to 20 (most intense)

>>Stress :

>>Overall Mood :

What are you grateful for today?

>>Tiredness :

>>Length of Sleeping (In hours) :

What would you like to do for yourself?
1. ___
2. ___
3. ___
4. ___

The present moment is filled with joy and happiness. If you are attentive, you will see it.
— Thich Nhat Hanh

My rewards for what has been successfully Done or just for the enjoyment of the day

My priorities for today
1. ___
2. ___
3. ___
4. ___

What inspired you today?

Did you have 5 minutes of stillness this morning?

☐ Yes   ☐ No

Did you realize a tense feeling during the day and after the experience of stillness this morning

☐ Yes   ☐ No

☐ Morning Routine   ☐ Evening Routine

My Plan to Enjoy My Day

Today's day and date: [M] [T] [W] [T] [F] [S] [S]   Day: [   ]   Month: [   ]   Year: [   ]

What did you enjoy most today?

Assign intensity on the scale from 1 to 20 (most intense)

>>Stress :

>>Overall Mood :

What are you grateful for today?

>>Tiredness :

>>Length of Sleeping (In hours) :

What would you like to do for yourself?
1.
2.
3.
4.

The present moment is filled with joy and happiness. If you are attentive, you will see it.
— Thich Nhat Hanh

My rewards for what has been successfully Done or just for the enjoyment of the day

My priorities for today
1.
2.
3.
4.

What inspired you today?

Did you have 5 minutes of stillness this morning?

[ ] Yes   [ ] No

Did you realize a tense feeling during the day and after the experience of stillness this morning

[ ] Yes   [ ] No

[ ] Morning Routine   [ ] Evening Routine

My Plan to Enjoy My Day

Today's day and date: [M] [T] [W] [T] [F] [S] [S]   Day: [　　]   Month: [　　]   Year: [　　]

What did you enjoy most today?

Assign intensity on the scale from 1 to 20 (most intense)

>>Stress :

>>Overall Mood :

What are you grateful for today?

>>Tiredness :

>>Length of Sleeping (In hours) :

What would you like to do for yourself?
1. ___
2. ___
3. ___
4. ___

The present moment is filled with joy and happiness. If you are attentive, you will see it.
— Thich Nhat Hanh

My rewards for what has been successfully Done or just for the enjoyment of the day

My priorities for today
1. ___
2. ___
3. ___
4. ___

What inspired you today?

Did you have 5 minutes of stillness this morning?

[ ] Yes   [ ] No

Did you realize a tense feeling during the day and after the experience of stillness this morning

[ ] Yes   [ ] No

[ ] Morning Routine   [ ] Evening Routine

My Plan to Enjoy My Day

Today's day and date: | M | T | W | T | F | S | S | Day: [   ]   Month: [   ]   Year: [   ]

What did you enjoy most today?

Assign intensity on the scale from 1 to 20 (most intense)

\>>Stress :

\>>Overall Mood :

What are you grateful for today?

\>>Tiredness :

\>>Length of Sleeping (In hours) :

What would you like to do for yourself?
1.
2.
3.
4.

The present moment is filled with joy and happiness. If you are attentive, you will see it.
— *Thich Nhat Hanh*

My rewards for what has been successfully Done or just for the enjoyment of the day

My priorities for today
1.
2.
3.
4.

What inspired you today?

Did you have 5 minutes of stillness this morning?

☐ Yes   ☐ No

Did you realize a tense feeling during the day and after the experience of stillness this morning

☐ Yes   ☐ No

☐ Morning Routine   ☐ Evening Routine

My Plan to Enjoy My Day

Today's day and date: [M] [T] [W] [T] [F] [S] [S] Day: [   ] Month: [   ] Year: [   ]

What did you enjoy most today?

Assign intensity on the scale from 1 to 20 (most intense)

>>Stress :

>>Overall Mood :

What are you grateful for today?

>>Tiredness :

>>Length of Sleeping (In hours) :

What would you like to do for yourself?
1. ___
2. ___
3. ___
4. ___

The present moment is filled with joy and happiness. If you are attentive, you will see it.
— Thich Nhat Hanh

My rewards for what has been successfully Done or just for the enjoyment of the day

My priorities for today
1. ___
2. ___
3. ___
4. ___

What inspired you today?

Did you have 5 minutes of stillness this morning?

☐ Yes   ☐ No

Did you realize a tense feeling during the day and after the experience of stillness this morning

☐ Yes   ☐ No

☐ Morning Routine   ☐ Evening Routine

My Plan to Enjoy My Day

Today's day and date: [M] [T] [W] [T] [F] [S] [S]   Day: [   ]   Month: [   ]   Year: [   ]

What did you enjoy most today?

Assign intensity on the scale from 1 to 20 (most intense)

>>Stress :

>>Overall Mood :

What are you grateful for today?

>>Tiredness :

>>Length of Sleeping (In hours) :

What would you like to do for yourself?
1.
2.
3.
4.

The present moment is filled with joy and happiness. If you are attentive, you will see it.
— Thich Nhat Hanh

My rewards for what has been successfully Done or just for the enjoyment of the day

My priorities for today
1.
2.
3.
4.

What inspired you today?

Did you have 5 minutes of stillness this morning?

☐ Yes   ☐ No

Did you realize a tense feeling during the day and after the experience of stillness this morning

☐ Yes   ☐ No

☐ Morning Routine   ☐ Evening Routine

My Plan to Enjoy My Day

Today's day and date: [M] [T] [W] [T] [F] [S] [S]   Day: [   ]   Month: [   ]   Year: [   ]

What did you enjoy most today?

Assign intensity on the scale from 1 to 20 (most intense)

>>Stress :

>>Overall Mood :

What are you grateful for today?

>>Tiredness :

>>Length of Sleeping (In hours) :

What would you like to do for yourself?
1.
2.
3.
4.

The present moment is filled with joy and happiness. If you are attentive, you will see it.
— Thich Nhat Hanh

My rewards for what has been successfully Done or just for the enjoyment of the day

My priorities for today
1.
2.
3.
4.

What inspired you today?

Did you have 5 minutes of stillness this morning?

☐ Yes   ☐ No

Did you realize a tense feeling during the day and after the experience of stillness this morning

☐ Yes   ☐ No

☐ Morning Routine   ☐ Evening Routine

My Plan For Fulfilling of My Life Dreams

What would I like to do?

1	
2	
3	
4	

Who is involved in my idea what to do?

1	
2	
3	
4	

What are my expectations?

1	
2	
3	
4	

Is that idea one of my life dreams?

1	☐ Yes	☐ No
2	☐ Yes	☐ No
3	☐ Yes	☐ No
4	☐ Yes	☐ No

Am I Felling Stress?

How intense is my stress on the scale from 1 to 20 (Most intense)	
Monday	
Tuesday	
Wednesday	
Thursday	
Friday	

Do I need to take a break?		
Monday	Yes	No
Tuesday	Yes	No
Wednesday	Yes	No
Thursday	Yes	No
Friday	Yes	No

If no, finishing your activity doesn't mean that you can relax, true?		
Monday	Yes	No
Tuesday	Yes	No
Wednesday	Yes	No
Thursday	Yes	No
Friday	Yes	No

Am I happy at this moment		
Monday	Yes	No
Tuesday	Yes	No
Wednesday	Yes	No
Thursday	Yes	No
Friday	Yes	No

If no, why is important to continue in my activity?		
Monday	Yes	No
Tuesday	Yes	No
Wednesday	Yes	No
Thursday	Yes	No
Friday	Yes	No

If no, do I want to be happy?		
Monday	Yes	No
Tuesday	Yes	No
Wednesday	Yes	No
Thursday	Yes	No
Friday	Yes	No

My Plan to Enjoy My Day

Today's day and date: [M] [T] [W] [T] [F] [S] [S] Day: [   ] Month: [   ] Year: [   ]

What did you enjoy most today?

Assign intensity on the scale from 1 to 20 (most intense)

>>Stress :

>>Overall Mood :

>>Tiredness :

What are you grateful for today?

>>Length of Sleeping (In hours) :

What would you like to do for yourself?
1.
2.
3.
4.

The present moment is filled with joy and happiness. If you are attentive, you will see it.
— Thich Nhat Hanh

My rewards for what has been successfully Done or just for the enjoyment of the day

My priorities for today
1.
2.
3.
4.

What inspired you today?

Did you have 5 minutes of stillness this morning?

[ ] Yes   [ ] No

Did you realize a tense feeling during the day and after the experience of stillness this morning

[ ] Yes   [ ] No

[ ] Morning Routine [ ] Evening Routine

My Plan to Enjoy My Day

Today's day and date: [M] [T] [W] [T] [F] [S] [S]   Day: [   ]   Month: [   ]   Year: [   ]

What did you enjoy most today?

Assign intensity on the scale from 1 to 20 (most intense)

>>Stress :

>>Overall Mood :

What are you grateful for today?

>>Tiredness :

>>Length of Sleeping (In hours) :

What would you like to do for yourself?
1.
2.
3.
4.

The present moment is filled with joy and happiness. If you are attentive, you will see it.
— Thich Nhat Hanh

My rewards for what has been successfully Done or just for the enjoyment of the day

My priorities for today
1.
2.
3.
4.

What inspired you today?

Did you have 5 minutes of stillness this morning?

☐ Yes   ☐ No

Did you realize a tense feeling during the day and after the experience of stillness this morning

☐ Yes   ☐ No

☐ Morning Routine   ☐ Evening Routine

My Plan to Enjoy My Day

Today's day and date: [M] [T] [W] [T] [F] [S] [S] Day: [   ] Month: [   ] Year: [   ]

What did you enjoy most today?

Assign intensity on the scale from 1 to 20 (most intense)

>>Stress :

>>Overall Mood :

What are you grateful for today?

>>Tiredness :

>>Length of Sleeping (In hours) :

What would you like to do for yourself?
1.
2.
3.
4.

The present moment is filled with joy and happiness. If you are attentive, you will see it.
— Thich Nhat Hanh

My rewards for what has been successfully Done or just for the enjoyment of the day

My priorities for today
1.
2.
3.
4.

What inspired you today?

Did you have 5 minutes of stillness this morning?

☐ Yes   ☐ No

Did you realize a tense feeling during the day and after the experience of stillness this morning

☐ Yes   ☐ No

☐ Morning Routine ☐ Evening Routine

My Plan to Enjoy My Day

Today's day and date: [M] [T] [W] [T] [F] [S] [S]   Day: [   ]   Month: [   ]   Year: [   ]

What did you enjoy most today?

Assign intensity on the scale from 1 to 20 (most intense)

>>Stress :

>>Overall Mood :

What are you grateful for today?

>>Tiredness :

>>Length of Sleeping (In hours) :

What would you like to do for yourself?
1. ___
2. ___
3. ___
4. ___

The present moment is filled with joy and happiness. If you are attentive, you will see it.
— Thich Nhat Hanh

My rewards for what has been successfully Done or just for the enjoyment of the day

My priorities for today
1. ___
2. ___
3. ___
4. ___

What inspired you today?

Did you have 5 minutes of stillness this morning?

☐ Yes   ☐ No

Did you realize a tense feeling during the day and after the experience of stillness this morning

☐ Yes   ☐ No

☐ Morning Routine   ☐ Evening Routine

My Plan to Enjoy My Day

Today's day and date: [M] [T] [W] [T] [F] [S] [S]   Day: [   ]   Month: [   ]   Year: [   ]

What did you enjoy most today?

Assign intensity on the scale from 1 to 20 (most intense)

>>Stress :

>>Overall Mood :

What are you grateful for today?

>>Tiredness :

>>Length of Sleeping (In hours) :

What would you like to do for yourself?
1.
2.
3.
4.

The present moment is filled with joy and happiness. If you are attentive, you will see it.
— Thich Nhat Hanh

My rewards for what has been successfully Done or just for the enjoyment of the day

My priorities for today
1.
2.
3.
4.

What inspired you today?

Did you have 5 minutes of stillness this morning?

[ ] Yes   [ ] No

Did you realize a tense feeling during the day and after the experience of stillness this morning

[ ] Yes   [ ] No

[ ] Morning Routine   [ ] Evening Routine

My Plan to Enjoy My Day

Today's day and date: [M] [T] [W] [T] [F] [S] [S] Day: [ ] Month: [ ] Year: [ ]

What did you enjoy most today?

Assign intensity on the scale from 1 to 20 (most intense)

>>Stress :

>>Overall Mood :

What are you grateful for today?

>>Tiredness :

>>Length of Sleeping (In hours) :

What would you like to do for yourself?
1.
2.
3.
4.

The present moment is filled with joy and happiness. If you are attentive, you will see it.
— Thich Nhat Hanh

My rewards for what has been successfully Done or just for the enjoyment of the day

My priorities for today
1.
2.
3.
4.

What inspired you today?

Did you have 5 minutes of stillness this morning?

[ ] Yes   [ ] No

Did you realize a tense feeling during the day and after the experience of stillness this morning

[ ] Yes   [ ] No

[ ] Morning Routine   [ ] Evening Routine

My Plan to Enjoy My Day

Today's day and date: [M] [T] [W] [T] [F] [S] [S] Day: [　] Month: [　] Year: [　]

What did you enjoy most today?

Assign intensity on the scale from 1 to 20 (most intense)

>>Stress :

>>Overall Mood :

What are you grateful for today?

>>Tiredness :

>>Length of Sleeping (In hours) :

What would you like to do for yourself?
1.
2.
3.
4.

The present moment is filled with joy and happiness. If you are attentive, you will see it.
— Thich Nhat Hanh

My rewards for what has been successfully Done or just for the enjoyment of the day

My priorities for today
1.
2.
3.
4.

What inspired you today?

Did you have 5 minutes of stillness this morning?

[ ] Yes   [ ] No

Did you realize a tense feeling during the day and after the experience of stillness this morning

[ ] Yes   [ ] No

[ ] Morning Routine [ ] Evening Routine

My Plan For Fulfilling of My Life Dreams

What would I like to do?

1	
2	
3	
4	

Who is involved in my idea what to do?

1	
2	
3	
4	

What are my expectations?

1	
2	
3	
4	

Is that idea one of my life dreams?

1	☐ Yes	☐ No
2	☐ Yes	☐ No
3	☐ Yes	☐ No
4	☐ Yes	☐ No

Am I Felling Stress?

How intense is my stress on the scale from 1 to 20 (Most intense)	
Monday	
Tuesday	
Wednesday	
Thursday	
Friday	

Do I need to take a break?		
Monday	Yes	No
Tuesday	Yes	No
Wednesday	Yes	No
Thursday	Yes	No
Friday	Yes	No

If no, finishing your activity doesn't mean that you can relax, true?		
Monday	Yes	No
Tuesday	Yes	No
Wednesday	Yes	No
Thursday	Yes	No
Friday	Yes	No

Am I happy at this moment		
Monday	Yes	No
Tuesday	Yes	No
Wednesday	Yes	No
Thursday	Yes	No
Friday	Yes	No

If no, why is important to continue in my activity?		
Monday	Yes	No
Tuesday	Yes	No
Wednesday	Yes	No
Thursday	Yes	No
Friday	Yes	No

If no, do I want to be happy?		
Monday	Yes	No
Tuesday	Yes	No
Wednesday	Yes	No
Thursday	Yes	No
Friday	Yes	No

My Plan to Enjoy My Day

Today's day and date: [M] [T] [W] [T] [F] [S] [S]   Day: [   ]   Month: [   ]   Year: [   ]

What did you enjoy most today?

Assign intensity on the scale from 1 to 20 (most intense)

>>Stress :

>>Overall Mood :

What are you grateful for today?

>>Tiredness :

>>Length of Sleeping (In hours) :

What would you like to do for yourself?
1.
2.
3.
4.

The present moment is filled with joy and happiness. If you are attentive, you will see it.
— Thich Nhat Hanh

My rewards for what has been successfully Done or just for the enjoyment of the day

My priorities for today
1.
2.
3.
4.

What inspired you today?

Did you have 5 minutes of stillness this morning?

[ ] Yes   [ ] No

Did you realize a tense feeling during the day and after the experience of stillness this morning

[ ] Yes   [ ] No

[ ] Morning Routine   [ ] Evening Routine

My Plan to Enjoy My Day

Today's day and date: [M] [T] [W] [T] [F] [S] [S] Day: [ ] Month: [ ] Year: [ ]

What did you enjoy most today?

Assign intensity on the scale from 1 to 20 (most intense)

>>Stress :

>>Overall Mood :

What are you grateful for today?

>>Tiredness :

>>Length of Sleeping (In hours) :

What would you like to do for yourself?
1.
2.
3.
4.

The present moment is filled with joy and happiness. If you are attentive, you will see it.
— Thich Nhat Hanh

My rewards for what has been successfully Done or just for the enjoyment of the day

My priorities for today
1.
2.
3.
4.

What inspired you today?

Did you have 5 minutes of stillness this morning?

[ ] Yes   [ ] No

Did you realize a tense feeling during the day and after the experience of stillness this morning

[ ] Yes   [ ] No

[ ] Morning Routine   [ ] Evening Routine

My Plan to Enjoy My Day

Today's day and date: [M] [T] [W] [T] [F] [S] [S] Day: [   ] Month: [   ] Year: [   ]

What did you enjoy most today?

Assign intensity on the scale from 1 to 20 (most intense)

>>Stress :

>>Overall Mood :

What are you grateful for today?

>>Tiredness :

>>Length of Sleeping (In hours) :

What would you like to do for yourself?
1.
2.
3.
4.

The present moment is filled with joy and happiness. If you are attentive, you will see it.
— Thich Nhat Hanh

My rewards for what has been successfully Done or just for the enjoyment of the day

My priorities for today
1.
2.
3.
4.

What inspired you today?

Did you have 5 minutes of stillness this morning?

[ ] Yes   [ ] No

Did you realize a tense feeling during the day and after the experience of stillness this morning

[ ] Yes   [ ] No

[ ] Morning Routine   [ ] Evening Routine

My Plan to Enjoy My Day

Today's day and date: [M] [T] [W] [T] [F] [S] [S] Day: [   ] Month: [   ] Year: [   ]

What did you enjoy most today?

Assign intensity on the scale from 1 to 20 (most intense)

>>Stress :

>>Overall Mood :

>>Tiredness :

What are you grateful for today?

>>Length of Sleeping (In hours) :

What would you like to do for yourself?
1.
2.
3.
4.

The present moment is filled with joy and happiness. If you are attentive, you will see it.
— Thich Nhat Hanh

My rewards for what has been successfully Done or just for the enjoyment of the day

My priorities for today
1.
2.
3.
4.

What inspired you today?

Did you have 5 minutes of stillness this morning?

[ ] Yes   [ ] No

Did you realize a tense feeling during the day and after the experience of stillness this morning

[ ] Yes   [ ] No

[ ] Morning Routine   [ ] Evening Routine

My Plan to Enjoy My Day

Today's day and date: [M] [T] [W] [T] [F] [S] [S]   Day: [   ]   Month: [   ]   Year: [   ]

What did you enjoy most today?

Assign intensity on the scale from 1 to 20 (most intense)

>>Stress :

>>Overall Mood :

What are you grateful for today?

>>Tiredness :

>>Length of Sleeping (In hours) :

What would you like to do for yourself?
1.
2.
3.
4.

The present moment is filled with joy and happiness. If you are attentive, you will see it.
— Thich Nhat Hanh

My rewards for what has been successfully Done or just for the enjoyment of the day

My priorities for today
1.
2.
3.
4.

What inspired you today?

Did you have 5 minutes of stillness this morning?

☐ Yes   ☐ No

Did you realize a tense feeling during the day and after the experience of stillness this morning

☐ Yes   ☐ No

☐ Morning Routine   ☐ Evening Routine

My Plan to Enjoy My Day

Today's day and date: [M] [T] [W] [T] [F] [S] [S] Day: [   ] Month: [   ] Year: [   ]

What did you enjoy most today?

Assign intensity on the scale from 1 to 20 (most intense)

\>>Stress :

\>>Overall Mood :

What are you grateful for today?

\>>Tiredness :

\>>Length of Sleeping (In hours) :

What would you like to do for yourself?

1.
2.
3.
4.

The present moment is filled with joy and happiness. If you are attentive, you will see it.
— Thich Nhat Hanh

My rewards for what has been successfully Done or just for the enjoyment of the day

My priorities for today

1.
2.
3.
4.

What inspired you today?

Did you have 5 minutes of stillness this morning?

[ ] Yes   [ ] No

Did you realize a tense feeling during the day and after the experience of stillness this morning

[ ] Yes   [ ] No

[ ] Morning Routine   [ ] Evening Routine

My Plan to Enjoy My Day

Today's day and date: [M] [T] [W] [T] [F] [S] [S]   Day: [ ]   Month: [ ]   Year: [ ]

What did you enjoy most today?

Assign intensity on the scale from 1 to 20 (most intense)

>>Stress :

>>Overall Mood :

What are you grateful for today?

>>Tiredness :

>>Length of Sleeping (In hours) :

What would you like to do for yourself?
1.
2.
3.
4.

The present moment is filled with joy and happiness. If you are attentive, you will see it.
— Thich Nhat Hanh

My rewards for what has been successfully Done or just for the enjoyment of the day

My priorities for today
1.
2.
3.
4.

What inspired you today?

Did you have 5 minutes of stillness this morning?

☐ Yes   ☐ No

Did you realize a tense feeling during the day and after the experience of stillness this morning

☐ Yes   ☐ No

☐ Morning Routine   ☐ Evening Routine

My Plan For Fulfilling of My Life Dreams

What would I like to do?

1	
2	
3	
4	

Who is involved in my idea what to do?

1	
2	
3	
4	

What are my expectations?

1	
2	
3	
4	

Is that idea one of my life dreams?

1	☐ Yes	☐ No
2	☐ Yes	☐ No
3	☐ Yes	☐ No
4	☐ Yes	☐ No

Am I Felling Stress?

How intense is my stress on the scale from 1 to 20 (Most intense)	
Monday	
Tuesday	
Wednesday	
Thursday	
Friday	

Do I need to take a break?		
Monday	Yes	No
Tuesday	Yes	No
Wednesday	Yes	No
Thursday	Yes	No
Friday	Yes	No

If no, finishing your activity doesn't mean that you can relax, true?		
Monday	Yes	No
Tuesday	Yes	No
Wednesday	Yes	No
Thursday	Yes	No
Friday	Yes	No

Am I happy at this moment		
Monday	Yes	No
Tuesday	Yes	No
Wednesday	Yes	No
Thursday	Yes	No
Friday	Yes	No

If no, why is important to continue in my activity?		
Monday	Yes	No
Tuesday	Yes	No
Wednesday	Yes	No
Thursday	Yes	No
Friday	Yes	No

If no, do I want to be happy?		
Monday	Yes	No
Tuesday	Yes	No
Wednesday	Yes	No
Thursday	Yes	No
Friday	Yes	No

My Plan to Enjoy My Day

Today's day and date: [M] [T] [W] [T] [F] [S] [S] Day: [   ] Month: [   ] Year: [   ]

What did you enjoy most today?

Assign intensity on the scale from 1 to 20 (most intense)

\>\>Stress :

\>\>Overall Mood :

What are you grateful for today?

\>\>Tiredness :

\>\>Length of Sleeping (In hours) :

What would you like to do for yourself?

1.
2.
3.
4.

The present moment is filled with joy and happiness. If you are attentive, you will see it.
— Thich Nhat Hanh

My rewards for what has been successfully Done or just for the enjoyment of the day

My priorities for today

1.
2.
3.
4.

What inspired you today?

Did you have 5 minutes of stillness this morning?

[ ] Yes [ ] No

Did you realize a tense feeling during the day and after the experience of stillness this morning

[ ] Yes [ ] No

[ ] Morning Routine [ ] Evening Routine

My Plan to Enjoy My Day

Today's day and date: [M] [T] [W] [T] [F] [S] [S]   Day: [   ]   Month: [   ]   Year: [   ]

What did you enjoy most today?

Assign intensity on the scale from 1 to 20 (most intense)

>>Stress :

>>Overall Mood :

What are you grateful for today?

>>Tiredness :

>>Length of Sleeping (In hours) :

What would you like to do for yourself?
1.
2.
3.
4.

The present moment is filled with joy and happiness. If you are attentive, you will see it.
Thich Nhat Hanh

My rewards for what has been successfully Done or just for the enjoyment of the day

My priorities for today
1.
2.
3.
4.

What inspired you today?

Did you have 5 minutes of stillness this morning?

☐ Yes   ☐ No

Did you realize a tense feeling during the day and after the experience of stillness this morning

☐ Yes   ☐ No

☐ Morning Routine   ☐ Evening Routine

My Plan to Enjoy My Day

Today's day and date: | M | T | W | T | F | S | S | Day: [   ]   Month: [   ]   Year: [   ]

What did you enjoy most today?

Assign intensity on the scale from 1 to 20 (most intense)

>>Stress :

>>Overall Mood :

What are you grateful for today?

>>Tiredness :

>>Length of Sleeping (In hours) :

What would you like to do for yourself?
1.
2.
3.
4.

The present moment is filled with joy and happiness. If you are attentive, you will see it.
— Thich Nhat Hanh

My rewards for what has been successfully Done or just for the enjoyment of the day

My priorities for today
1.
2.
3.
4.

What inspired you today?

Did you have 5 minutes of stillness this morning?

☐ Yes   ☐ No

Did you realize a tense feeling during the day and after the experience of stillness this morning

☐ Yes   ☐ No

☐ Morning Routine   ☐ Evening Routine

My Plan to Enjoy My Day

Today's day and date: [M] [T] [W] [T] [F] [S] [S] Day: [   ] Month: [   ] Year: [   ]

What did you enjoy most today?

Assign intensity on the scale from 1 to 20 (most intense)

>>Stress :

>>Overall Mood :

What are you grateful for today?

>>Tiredness :

>>Length of Sleeping (In hours) :

What would you like to do for yourself?
1. _____
2. _____
3. _____
4. _____

The present moment is filled with joy and happiness. If you are attentive, you will see it.
— Thich Nhat Hanh

My rewards for what has been successfully Done or just for the enjoyment of the day

My priorities for today
1. _____
2. _____
3. _____
4. _____

What inspired you today?

Did you have 5 minutes of stillness this morning?

☐ Yes   ☐ No

Did you realize a tense feeling during the day and after the experience of stillness this morning

☐ Yes   ☐ No

☐ Morning Routine   ☐ Evening Routine

My Plan to Enjoy My Day

Today's day and date: [M] [T] [W] [T] [F] [S] [S]   Day: _____   Month: _____   Year: _____

What did you enjoy most today?

Assign intensity on the scale from 1 to 20 (most intense)

>>Stress : _____

>>Overall Mood : _____

What are you grateful for today?

>>Tiredness : _____

>>Length of Sleeping (In hours) : _____

What would you like to do for yourself?
1. _____
2. _____
3. _____
4. _____

The present moment is filled with joy and happiness. If you are attentive, you will see it.
— Thich Nhat Hanh

My rewards for what has been successfully Done or just for the enjoyment of the day

My priorities for today
1. _____
2. _____
3. _____
4. _____

What inspired you today?

Did you have 5 minutes of stillness this morning?

☐ Yes   ☐ No

Did you realize a tense feeling during the day and after the experience of stillness this morning

☐ Yes   ☐ No

☐ Morning Routine   ☐ Evening Routine

My Plan to Enjoy My Day

Today's day and date: [M] [T] [W] [T] [F] [S] [S] Day: [   ] Month: [   ] Year: [   ]

What did you enjoy most today?

Assign intensity on the scale from 1 to 20 (most intense)

>>Stress :

>>Overall Mood :

What are you grateful for today?

>>Tiredness :

>>Length of Sleeping (In hours) :

What would you like to do for yourself?
1.
2.
3.
4.

The present moment is filled with joy and happiness. If you are attentive, you will see it.

Thich Nhat Hanh

My rewards for what has been successfully Done or just for the enjoyment of the day

My priorities for today
1.
2.
3.
4.

What inspired you today?

Did you have 5 minutes of stillness this morning?

[ ] Yes [ ] No

Did you realize a tense feeling during the day and after the experience of stillness this morning

[ ] Yes [ ] No

[ ] Morning Routine [ ] Evening Routine

My Plan to Enjoy My Day

Today's day and date: [M] [T] [W] [T] [F] [S] [S]   Day: [   ]   Month: [   ]   Year: [   ]

What did you enjoy most today?

Assign intensive on the scale from 1 to 20 (most intense)

>>Stress :

>>Overall Mood :

What are you grateful for today?

>>Tiredness :

>>Length of Sleeping (In hours) :

What would you like to do for yourself?

1.
2.
3.
4.

The present moment is filled with joy and happiness. If you are attentive, you will see it.

— Thich Nhat Hanh

My rewards for what has been successfully Done or just for the enjoyment of the day

My priorities for today

1.
2.
3.
4.

What inspired you today?

Did you have 5 minutes of stillness this morning?

☐ Yes   ☐ No

Did you realize a tense feeling during the day and after the experience of stillness this morning

☐ Yes   ☐ No

☐ Morning Routine   ☐ Evening Routine

My Plan For Fulfilling of My Life Dreams

What would I like to do?

1	
2	
3	
4	

Who is involved in my idea what to do?

1	
2	
3	
4	

What are my expectations?

1	
2	
3	
4	

Is that idea one of my life dreams?

1	☐ Yes	☐ No
2	☐ Yes	☐ No
3	☐ Yes	☐ No
4	☐ Yes	☐ No

Am I Felling Stress?

How intense is my stress on the scale from 1 to 20 (Most intense)	
Monday	
Tuesday	
Wednesday	
Thursday	
Friday	

Do I need to take a break?		
Monday	Yes	No
Tuesday	Yes	No
Wednesday	Yes	No
Thursday	Yes	No
Friday	Yes	No

If no, finishing your activity doesn't mean that you can relax, true?		
Monday	Yes	No
Tuesday	Yes	No
Wednesday	Yes	No
Thursday	Yes	No
Friday	Yes	No

Am I happy at this moment		
Monday	Yes	No
Tuesday	Yes	No
Wednesday	Yes	No
Thursday	Yes	No
Friday	Yes	No

If no, why is important to continue in my activity?		
Monday	Yes	No
Tuesday	Yes	No
Wednesday	Yes	No
Thursday	Yes	No
Friday	Yes	No

If no, do I want to be happy?		
Monday	Yes	No
Tuesday	Yes	No
Wednesday	Yes	No
Thursday	Yes	No
Friday	Yes	No

My Plan to Enjoy My Day

Today's day and date: [M] [T] [W] [T] [F] [S] [S]   Day: [ ]   Month: [ ]   Year: [ ]

What did you enjoy most today?

Assign intensity on the scale from 1 to 20 (most intense)

>>Stress :

>>Overall Mood :

What are you grateful for today?

>>Tiredness :

>>Length of Sleeping (In hours) :

What would you like to do for yourself?
1.
2.
3.
4.

The present moment is filled with joy and happiness. If you are attentive, you will see it.
— Thich Nhat Hanh

My rewards for what has been successfully Done or just for the enjoyment of the day

My priorities for today
1.
2.
3.
4.

What inspired you today?

Did you have 5 minutes of stillness this morning?

[ ] Yes   [ ] No

Did you realize a tense feeling during the day and after the experience of stillness this morning

[ ] Yes   [ ] No

[ ] Morning Routine   [ ] Evening Routine

My Plan to Enjoy My Day

Today's day and date: [M] [T] [W] [T] [F] [S] [S] Day: [ ] Month: [ ] Year: [ ]

What did you enjoy most today?

Assign intensity on the scale from 1 to 20 (most intense)

>>Stress :

>>Overall Mood :

What are you grateful for today?

>>Tiredness :

>>Length of Sleeping (In hours) :

What would you like to do for yourself?

1.
2.
3.
4.

The present moment is filled with joy and happiness. If you are attentive, you will see it.

Thich Nhat Hanh

My rewards for what has been successfully Done or just for the enjoyment of the day

My priorities for today

1.
2.
3.
4.

What inspired you today?

Did you have 5 minutes of stillness this morning?

[ ] Yes   [ ] No

Did you realize a tense feeling during the day and after the experience of stillness this morning

[ ] Yes   [ ] No

[ ] Morning Routine   [ ] Evening Routine

My Plan to Enjoy My Day

Today's day and date: [M] [T] [W] [T] [F] [S] [S] Day: [   ] Month: [   ] Year: [   ]

What did you enjoy most today?

Assign intensity on the scale from 1 to 20 (most intense)

>>Stress :

>>Overall Mood :

What are you grateful for today?

>>Tiredness :

>>Length of Sleeping (In hours) :

What would you like to do for yourself?
1.
2.
3.
4.

The present moment is filled with joy and happiness. If you are attentive, you will see it.
Thich Nhat Hanh

My rewards for what has been successfully Done or just for the enjoyment of the day

My priorities for today
1.
2.
3.
4.

What inspired you today?

Did you have 5 minutes of stillness this morning?

[ ] Yes   [ ] No

Did you realize a tense feeling during the day and after the experience of stillness this morning

[ ] Yes   [ ] No

[ ] Morning Routine   [ ] Evening Routine

My Plan to Enjoy My Day

Today's day and date: [M] [T] [W] [T] [F] [S] [S]   Day: [   ]   Month: [   ]   Year: [   ]

What did you enjoy most today?

Assign intensity on the scale from 1 to 20 (most intense)

>>Stress :

>>Overall Mood :

>>Tiredness :

What are you grateful for today?

>>Length of Sleeping (In hours) :

What would you like to do for yourself?

1.
2.
3.
4.

The present moment is filled with joy and happiness. If you are attentive, you will see it.
— Thich Nhat Hanh

My rewards for what has been successfully Done or just for the enjoyment of the day

My priorities for today

1.
2.
3.
4.

What inspired you today?

Did you have 5 minutes of stillness this morning?

[ ] Yes   [ ] No

Did you realize a tense feeling during the day and after the experience of stillness this morning

[ ] Yes   [ ] No

[ ] Morning Routine [ ] Evening Routine

My Plan to Enjoy My Day

Today's day and date: [M] [T] [W] [T] [F] [S] [S]   Day: [ ]   Month: [ ]   Year: [ ]

What did you enjoy most today?

Assign intensity on the scale from 1 to 20 (most intense)

>>Stress :

>>Overall Mood :

What are you grateful for today?

>>Tiredness :

>>Length of Sleeping (In hours) :

What would you like to do for yourself?
1.
2.
3.
4.

The present moment is filled with joy and happiness. If you are attentive, you will see it.
Thich Nhat Hanh

My rewards for what has been successfully Done or just for the enjoyment of the day

My priorities for today
1.
2.
3.
4.

What inspired you today?

Did you have 5 minutes of stillness this morning?

[ ] Yes   [ ] No

Did you realize a tense feeling during the day and after the experience of stillness this morning

[ ] Yes   [ ] No

[ ] Morning Routine   [ ] Evening Routine

My Plan to Enjoy My Day

Today's day and date: | M | T | W | T | F | S | S | Day: [   ]   Month: [   ]   Year: [   ]

What did you enjoy most today?

Assign intensity on the scale from 1 to 20 (most intense)

>>Stress :

>>Overall Mood :

>>Tiredness :

What are you grateful for today?

>>Length of Sleeping (In hours) :

What would you like to do for yourself?
1.
2.
3.
4.

The present moment is filled with joy and happiness. If you are attentive, you will see it.
— Thich Nhat Hanh

My rewards for what has been successfully Done or just for the enjoyment of the day

My priorities for today
1.
2.
3.
4.

What inspired you today?

Did you have 5 minutes of stillness this morning?

☐ Yes   ☐ No

Did you realize a tense feeling during the day and after the experience of stillness this morning

☐ Yes   ☐ No

☐ Morning Routine   ☐ Evening Routine

My Plan to Enjoy My Day

Today's day and date: [M] [T] [W] [T] [F] [S] [S]   Day: [ ]   Month: [ ]   Year: [ ]

What did you enjoy most today?

Assign intensity on the scale from 1 to 20 (most intense)

>>Stress :

>>Overall Mood :

What are you grateful for today?

>>Tiredness :

>>Length of Sleeping (In hours) :

What would you like to do for yourself?
1.
2.
3.
4.

The present moment is filled with joy and happiness. If you are attentive, you will see it.
— Thich Nhat Hanh

My rewards for what has been successfully Done or just for the enjoyment of the day

My priorities for today
1.
2.
3.
4.

What inspired you today?

Did you have 5 minutes of stillness this morning?

☐ Yes   ☐ No

Did you realize a tense feeling during the day and after the experience of stillness this morning

☐ Yes   ☐ No

☐ Morning Routine   ☐ Evening Routine

My Plan For Fulfilling of My Life Dreams

What would I like to do?

1	
2	
3	
4	

Who is involved in my idea what to do?

1	
2	
3	
4	

What are my expectations?

1	
2	
3	
4	

Is that idea one of my life dreams?

1	☐ Yes	☐ No
2	☐ Yes	☐ No
3	☐ Yes	☐ No
4	☐ Yes	☐ No

Am I Felling *Stress?*

How intense is my stress on the scale from 1 to 20 (Most intense)	
Monday	
Tuesday	
Wednesday	
Thursday	
Friday	

Do I need to take a break?		
Monday	Yes	No
Tuesday	Yes	No
Wednesday	Yes	No
Thursday	Yes	No
Friday	Yes	No

If no, finishing your activity doesn't mean that you can relax, true?		
Monday	Yes	No
Tuesday	Yes	No
Wednesday	Yes	No
Thursday	Yes	No
Friday	Yes	No

Am I happy at this moment		
Monday	Yes	No
Tuesday	Yes	No
Wednesday	Yes	No
Thursday	Yes	No
Friday	Yes	No

If no, why is important to continue in my activity?		
Monday	Yes	No
Tuesday	Yes	No
Wednesday	Yes	No
Thursday	Yes	No
Friday	Yes	No

If no, do I want to be happy?		
Monday	Yes	No
Tuesday	Yes	No
Wednesday	Yes	No
Thursday	Yes	No
Friday	Yes	No

My Plan to Enjoy My Day

Today's day and date: | M | T | W | T | F | S | S | Day: [   ]   Month: [   ]   Year: [   ]

What did you enjoy most today?

Assign intensity on the scale from 1 to 20 (most intense)

>>Stress :

>>Overall Mood :

What are you grateful for today?

>>Tiredness :

>>Length of Sleeping (In hours) :

What would you like to do for yourself?
1.
2.
3.
4.

> The present moment is filled with joy and happiness. If you are attentive, you will see it.
> Thich Nhat Hanh

My rewards for what has been successfully Done or just for the enjoyment of the day

My priorities for today
1.
2.
3.
4.

What inspired you today?

Did you have 5 minutes of stillness this morning?

☐ Yes   ☐ No

Did you realize a tense feeling during the day and after the experience of stillness this morning

☐ Yes   ☐ No

☐ Morning Routine   ☐ Evening Routine

My Plan to Enjoy My Day

Today's day and date: [M] [T] [W] [T] [F] [S] [S] Day: [ ] Month: [ ] Year: [ ]

What did you enjoy most today?

Assign intensity on the scale from 1 to 20 (most intense)

>>Stress :

>>Overall Mood :

What are you grateful for today?

>>Tiredness :

>>Length of Sleeping (In hours) :

What would you like to do for yourself?
1.
2.
3.
4.

The present moment is filled with joy and happiness. If you are attentive, you will see it.
— Thich Nhat Hanh

My rewards for what has been successfully Done or just for the enjoyment of the day

My priorities for today
1.
2.
3.
4.

What inspired you today?

Did you have 5 minutes of stillness this morning?

[ ] Yes   [ ] No

Did you realize a tense feeling during the day and after the experience of stillness this morning

[ ] Yes   [ ] No

[ ] Morning Routine [ ] Evening Routine

My Plan to Enjoy My Day

Today's day and date: [M] [T] [W] [T] [F] [S] [S]   Day: [   ]   Month: [   ]   Year: [   ]

What did you enjoy most today?

Assign intensity on the scale from 1 to 20 (most intense)

>>Stress :

>>Overall Mood :

What are you grateful for today?

>>Tiredness :

>>Length of Sleeping (In hours) :

What would you like to do for yourself?
1.
2.
3.
4.

> The present moment is filled with joy and happiness. If you are attentive, you will see it.
> — Thich Nhat Hanh

My rewards for what has been successfully Done or just for the enjoyment of the day

My priorities for today
1.
2.
3.
4.

What inspired you today?

Did you have 5 minutes of stillness this morning?

☐ Yes   ☐ No

Did you realize a tense feeling during the day and after the experience of stillness this morning

☐ Yes   ☐ No

☐ Morning Routine   ☐ Evening Routine

My Plan to Enjoy My Day

Today's day and date: | M | T | W | T | F | S | S | Day: [   ]   Month: [   ]   Year: [   ]

What did you enjoy most today?

Assign intensity on the scale from 1 to 20 (most intense)

>>Stress :

>>Overall Mood :

What are you grateful for today?

>>Tiredness :

>>Length of Sleeping (In hours) :

What would you like to do for yourself?
1.
2.
3.
4.

The present moment is filled with joy and happiness. If you are attentive, you will see it.
— Thich Nhat Hanh

My rewards for what has been successfully Done or just for the enjoyment of the day

My priorities for today
1.
2.
3.
4.

What inspired you today?

Did you have 5 minutes of stillness this morning?

☐ Yes   ☐ No

Did you realize a tense feeling during the day and after the experience of stillness this morning

☐ Yes   ☐ No

☐ Morning Routine   ☐ Evening Routine

My Plan to Enjoy My Day

Today's day and date: [M] [T] [W] [T] [F] [S] [S]   Day: [   ]   Month: [   ]   Year: [   ]

What did you enjoy most today?

Assign intensity on the scale from 1 to 20 (most intense)

>>Stress :

>>Overall Mood :

>>Tiredness :

What are you grateful for today?

>>Length of Sleeping (In hours) :

What would you like to do for yourself?
1.
2.
3.
4.

The present moment is filled with joy and happiness. If you are attentive, you will see it.
— Thich Nhat Hanh

My rewards for what has been successfully Done or just for the enjoyment of the day

My priorities for today
1.
2.
3.
4.

What inspired you today?

Did you have 5 minutes of stillness this morning?

☐ Yes   ☐ No

Did you realize a tense feeling during the day and after the experience of stillness this morning

☐ Yes   ☐ No

☐ Morning Routine   ☐ Evening Routine

My Plan to Enjoy My Day

Today's day and date: [M] [T] [W] [T] [F] [S] [S]   Day: [   ]   Month: [   ]   Year: [   ]

What did you enjoy most today?

Assign intensity on the scale from 1 to 20 (most intense)

>>Stress :

>>Overall Mood :

What are you grateful for today?

>>Tiredness :

>>Length of Sleeping (In hours) :

What would you like to do for yourself?
1.
2.
3.
4.

The present moment is filled with joy and happiness. If you are attentive, you will see it.
— Thich Nhat Hanh

My rewards for what has been successfully Done or just for the enjoyment of the day

My priorities for today
1.
2.
3.
4.

What inspired you today?

Did you have 5 minutes of stillness this morning?

[ ] Yes   [ ] No

Did you realize a tense feeling during the day and after the experience of stillness this morning

[ ] Yes   [ ] No

[ ] Morning Routine   [ ] Evening Routine

My Plan to Enjoy My Day

Today's day and date: | M | T | W | T | F | S | S | Day: [   ]   Month: [   ]   Year: [   ]

What did you enjoy most today?

Assign intensity on the scale from 1 to 20 (most intense)

>>Stress :

>>Overall Mood :

What are you grateful for today?

>>Tiredness :

>>Length of Sleeping (In hours) :

What would you like to do for yourself?
1.
2.
3.
4.

The present moment is filled with joy and happiness. If you are attentive, you will see it.
— Thich Nhat Hanh

My rewards for what has been successfully Done or just for the enjoyment of the day

My priorities for today
1.
2.
3.
4.

What inspired you today?

Did you have 5 minutes of stillness this morning?

☐ Yes   ☐ No

Did you realize a tense feeling during the day and after the experience of stillness this morning

☐ Yes   ☐ No

☐ Morning Routine ☐ Evening Routine

My Plan For Fulfilling of My Life Dreams

What would I like to do?

1	
2	
3	
4	

Who is involved in my idea what to do?

1	
2	
3	
4	

What are my expectations?

1	
2	
3	
4	

Is that idea one of my life dreams?

1	☐ Yes	☐ No
2	☐ Yes	☐ No
3	☐ Yes	☐ No
4	☐ Yes	☐ No

Am I Felling Stress?

How intense is my stress on the scale from 1 to 20 (Most intense)	
Monday	
Tuesday	
Wednesday	
Thursday	
Friday	

Do I need to take a break?		
Monday	Yes	No
Tuesday	Yes	No
Wednesday	Yes	No
Thursday	Yes	No
Friday	Yes	No

If no, finishing your activity doesn't mean that you can relax, true?		
Monday	Yes	No
Tuesday	Yes	No
Wednesday	Yes	No
Thursday	Yes	No
Friday	Yes	No

Am I happy at this moment		
Monday	Yes	No
Tuesday	Yes	No
Wednesday	Yes	No
Thursday	Yes	No
Friday	Yes	No

If no, why is important to continue in my activity?		
Monday	Yes	No
Tuesday	Yes	No
Wednesday	Yes	No
Thursday	Yes	No
Friday	Yes	No

If no, do I want to be happy?		
Monday	Yes	No
Tuesday	Yes	No
Wednesday	Yes	No
Thursday	Yes	No
Friday	Yes	No

My Plan to Enjoy My Day

Today's day and date: [M] [T] [W] [T] [F] [S] [S] Day: [   ] Month: [   ] Year: [   ]

What did you enjoy most today?

Assign intensity on the scale from 1 to 20 (most intense)

>>Stress :

>>Overall Mood :

What are you grateful for today?

>>Tiredness :

>>Length of Sleeping (In hours) :

What would you like to do for yourself?
1. _____
2. _____
3. _____
4. _____

The present moment is filled with joy and happiness. If you are attentive, you will see it.
— Thich Nhat Hanh

My rewards for what has been successfully Done or just for the enjoyment of the day

My priorities for today
1. _____
2. _____
3. _____
4. _____

What inspired you today?

Did you have 5 minutes of stillness this morning?

☐ Yes   ☐ No

Did you realize a tense feeling during the day and after the experience of stillness this morning

☐ Yes   ☐ No

☐ Morning Routine   ☐ Evening Routine

My Plan to Enjoy My Day

Today's day and date: [M] [T] [W] [T] [F] [S] [S] Day: [   ] Month: [   ] Year: [   ]

What did you enjoy most today?

Assign intensity on the scale from 1 to 20 (most intense)

>>Stress :

>>Overall Mood :

What are you grateful for today?

>>Tiredness :

>>Length of Sleeping (In hours) :

What would you like to do for yourself?

1.
2.
3.
4.

> The present moment is filled with joy and happiness. If you are attentive, you will see it.
> — Thich Nhat Hanh

My rewards for what has been successfully Done or just for the enjoyment of the day

My priorities for today

1.
2.
3.
4.

What inspired you today?

Did you have 5 minutes of stillness this morning?

[ ] Yes   [ ] No

Did you realize a tense feeling during the day and after the experience of stillness this morning

[ ] Yes   [ ] No

[ ] Morning Routine   [ ] Evening Routine

My Plan to Enjoy My Day

Today's day and date: [M] [T] [W] [T] [F] [S] [S]　Day: [   ]　Month: [   ]　Year: [   ]

What did you enjoy most today?

Assign intensity on the scale from 1 to 20 (most intense)

>>Stress :

>>Overall Mood :

>>Tiredness :

What are you grateful for today?

>>Length of Sleeping (In hours) :

What would you like to do for yourself?
1.
2.
3.
4.

The present moment is filled with joy and happiness. If you are attentive, you will see it.

— Thich Nhat Hanh

My rewards for what has been successfully Done or just for the enjoyment of the day

My priorities for today
1.
2.
3.
4.

What inspired you today?

Did you have 5 minutes of stillness this morning?

[ ] Yes　　[ ] No

Did you realize a tense feeling during the day and after the experience of stillness this morning

[ ] Yes　　[ ] No

[ ] Morning Routine　[ ] Evening Routine

My Plan to Enjoy My Day

Today's day and date: | M | T | W | T | F | S | S | Day: [   ]   Month: [   ]   Year: [   ]

What did you enjoy most today?

Assign intensity on the scale from 1 to 20 (most intense)

\>\>Stress :

\>\>Overall Mood :

What are you grateful for today?

\>\>Tiredness :

\>\>Length of Sleeping (In hours) :

What would you like to do for yourself?
1.
2.
3.
4.

The present moment is filled with joy and happiness. If you are attentive, you will see it.
— Thich Nhat Hanh

My rewards for what has been successfully Done or just for the enjoyment of the day

My priorities for today
1.
2.
3.
4.

What inspired you today?

Did you have 5 minutes of stillness this morning?

☐ Yes   ☐ No

Did you realize a tense feeling during the day and after the experience of stillness this morning

☐ Yes   ☐ No

☐ Morning Routine   ☐ Evening Routine

My Plan to Enjoy My Day

Today's day and date: [M] [T] [W] [T] [F] [S] [S] Day: [ ] Month: [ ] Year: [ ]

What did you enjoy most today?

Assign intensity on the scale from 1 to 20 (most intense)

>>Stress :

>>Overall Mood :

What are you grateful for today?

>>Tiredness :

>>Length of Sleeping (In hours) :

What would you like to do for yourself?
1.
2.
3.
4.

The present moment is filled with joy and happiness. If you are attentive, you will see it.
Thich Nhat Hanh

My rewards for what has been successfully Done or just for the enjoyment of the day

My priorities for today
1.
2.
3.
4.

What inspired you today?

Did you have 5 minutes of stillness this morning?

[ ] Yes   [ ] No

Did you realize a tense feeling during the day and after the experience of stillness this morning

[ ] Yes   [ ] No

[ ] Morning Routine [ ] Evening Routine

My Plan to Enjoy My Day

Today's day and date: [M] [T] [W] [T] [F] [S] [S] Day: [ ] Month: [ ] Year: [ ]

What did you enjoy most today?

Assign intensity on the scale from 1 to 20 (most intense)

>>Stress :

>>Overall Mood :

>>Tiredness :

What are you grateful for today?

>>Length of Sleeping (In hours) :

What would you like to do for yourself?
1.
2.
3.
4.

The present moment is filled with joy and happiness. If you are attentive, you will see it.
Thich Nhat Hanh

My rewards for what has been successfully Done or just for the enjoyment of the day

My priorities for today
1.
2.
3.
4.

What inspired you today?

Did you have 5 minutes of stillness this morning?

☐ Yes   ☐ No

Did you realize a tense feeling during the day and after the experience of stillness this morning

☐ Yes   ☐ No

☐ Morning Routine   ☐ Evening Routine

My Plan to Enjoy My Day

Today's day and date: [M] [T] [W] [T] [F] [S] [S]   Day: [   ]   Month: [   ]   Year: [   ]

What did you enjoy most today?

Assign intensity on the scale from 1 to 20 (most intense)

>>Stress :

>>Overall Mood :

What are you grateful for today?

>>Tiredness :

>>Length of Sleeping (In hours) :

What would you like to do for yourself?
1. ___
2. ___
3. ___
4. ___

The present moment is filled with joy and happiness. If you are attentive, you will see it.
— Thich Nhat Hanh

My rewards for what has been successfully Done or just for the enjoyment of the day

My priorities for today
1. ___
2. ___
3. ___
4. ___

What inspired you today?

Did you have 5 minutes of stillness this morning?

[ ] Yes   [ ] No

Did you realize a tense feeling during the day and after the experience of stillness this morning

[ ] Yes   [ ] No

[ ] Morning Routine   [ ] Evening Routine

My Plan For Fulfilling of My Life Dreams

What would I like to do?

1	
2	
3	
4	

Who is involved in my idea what to do?

1	
2	
3	
4	

What are my expectations?

1	
2	
3	
4	

Is that idea one of my life dreams?

1	☐ Yes	☐ No
2	☐ Yes	☐ No
3	☐ Yes	☐ No
4	☐ Yes	☐ No

Am I Felling Stress?

How intense is my stress on the scale from 1 to 20 (Most intense)	
Monday	
Tuesday	
Wednesday	
Thursday	
Friday	

Do I need to take a break?		
Monday	Yes	No
Tuesday	Yes	No
Wednesday	Yes	No
Thursday	Yes	No
Friday	Yes	No

If no, finishing your activity doesn't mean that you can relax, true?		
Monday	Yes	No
Tuesday	Yes	No
Wednesday	Yes	No
Thursday	Yes	No
Friday	Yes	No

Am I happy at this moment		
Monday	Yes	No
Tuesday	Yes	No
Wednesday	Yes	No
Thursday	Yes	No
Friday	Yes	No

If no, why is important to continue in my activity?		
Monday	Yes	No
Tuesday	Yes	No
Wednesday	Yes	No
Thursday	Yes	No
Friday	Yes	No

If no, do I want to be happy?		
Monday	Yes	No
Tuesday	Yes	No
Wednesday	Yes	No
Thursday	Yes	No
Friday	Yes	No

My Plan to Enjoy My Day

Today's day and date: | M | T | W | T | F | S | S | Day: [   ]   Month: [   ]   Year: [   ]

What did you enjoy most today?

Assign intensity on the scale from 1 to 20 (most intense)

\>\>Stress :

\>\>Overall Mood :

\>\>Tiredness :

What are you grateful for today?

\>\>Length of Sleeping (In hours) :

What would you like to do for yourself?
1.
2.
3.
4.

The present moment is filled with joy and happiness. If you are attentive, you will see it.
Thich Nhat Hanh

My rewards for what has been successfully Done or just for the enjoyment of the day

My priorities for today
1.
2.
3.
4.

What inspired you today?

Did you have 5 minutes of stillness this morning?

☐ Yes   ☐ No

Did you realize a tense feeling during the day and after the experience of stillness this morning

☐ Yes   ☐ No

☐ Morning Routine   ☐ Evening Routine

My Plan to Enjoy My Day

Today's day and date: [M] [T] [W] [T] [F] [S] [S] Day: [ ] Month: [ ] Year: [ ]

What did you enjoy most today?

Assign intensity on the scale from 1 to 20 (most intense)

>>Stress :

>>Overall Mood :

What are you grateful for today?

>>Tiredness :

>>Length of Sleeping (In hours) :

What would you like to do for yourself?
1.
2.
3.
4.

The present moment is filled with joy and happiness. If you are attentive, you will see it.
— Thich Nhat Hanh

My rewards for what has been successfully Done or just for the enjoyment of the day

My priorities for today
1.
2.
3.
4.

What inspired you today?

Did you have 5 minutes of stillness this morning?

[ ] Yes   [ ] No

Did you realize a tense feeling during the day and after the experience of stillness this morning

[ ] Yes   [ ] No

[ ] Morning Routine   [ ] Evening Routine

My Plan to Enjoy My Day

Today's day and date: | M | T | W | T | F | S | S | Day: [   ]   Month: [   ]   Year: [   ]

What did you enjoy most today?

Assign intensity on the scale from 1 to 20 (most intense)

>>Stress :

>>Overall Mood :

>>Tiredness :

What are you grateful for today?

>>Length of Sleeping (In hours) :

What would you like to do for yourself?
1.
2.
3.
4.

The present moment is filled with joy and happiness. If you are attentive, you will see it.
— Thich Nhat Hanh

My rewards for what has been successfully Done or just for the enjoyment of the day

My priorities for today
1.
2.
3.
4.

What inspired you today?

Did you have 5 minutes of stillness this morning?

☐ Yes   ☐ No

Did you realize a tense feeling during the day and after the experience of stillness this morning

☐ Yes   ☐ No

☐ Morning Routine ☐ Evening Routine

My Plan to Enjoy My Day

Today's day and date: [M] [T] [W] [T] [F] [S] [S] Day: [ ] Month: [ ] Year: [ ]

What did you enjoy most today?

Assign intensity on the scale from 1 to 20 (most intense)

>>Stress :

>>Overall Mood :

What are you grateful for today?

>>Tiredness :

>>Length of Sleeping (In hours) :

What would you like to do for yourself?
1.
2.
3.
4.

The present moment is filled with joy and happiness. If you are attentive, you will see it.
— Thich Nhat Hanh

My rewards for what has been successfully Done or just for the enjoyment of the day

My priorities for today
1.
2.
3.
4.

What inspired you today?

Did you have 5 minutes of stillness this morning?

[ ] Yes   [ ] No

Did you realize a tense feeling during the day and after the experience of stillness this morning

[ ] Yes   [ ] No

[ ] Morning Routine [ ] Evening Routine

My Plan to Enjoy My Day

Today's day and date: [M] [T] [W] [T] [F] [S] [S] Day: [   ] Month: [   ] Year: [   ]

What did you enjoy most today?

Assign intensity on the scale from 1 to 20 (most intense)

>>Stress :

>>Overall Mood :

What are you grateful for today?

>>Tiredness :

>>Length of Sleeping (In hours) :

What would you like to do for yourself?
1.
2.
3.
4.

The present moment is filled with joy and happiness. If you are attentive, you will see it.
— Thich Nhat Hanh

My rewards for what has been successfully Done or just for the enjoyment of the day

My priorities for today
1.
2.
3.
4.

What inspired you today?

Did you have 5 minutes of stillness this morning?

[ ] Yes   [ ] No

Did you realize a tense feeling during the day and after the experience of stillness this morning

[ ] Yes   [ ] No

[ ] Morning Routine   [ ] Evening Routine

My Plan to Enjoy My Day

Today's day and date: [M] [T] [W] [T] [F] [S] [S] Day: [   ] Month: [   ] Year: [   ]

What did you enjoy most today?

Assign intensity on the scale from 1 to 20 (most intense)

>>Stress :

>>Overall Mood :

>>Tiredness :

What are you grateful for today?

>>Length of Sleeping (In hours) :

What would you like to do for yourself?
1.
2.
3.
4.

The present moment is filled with joy and happiness. If you are attentive, you will see it.

— Thich Nhat Hanh

My rewards for what has been successfully Done or just for the enjoyment of the day

My priorities for today
1.
2.
3.
4.

What inspired you today?

Did you have 5 minutes of stillness this morning?

[ ] Yes   [ ] No

Did you realize a tense feeling during the day and after the experience of stillness this morning

[ ] Yes   [ ] No

[ ] Morning Routine   [ ] Evening Routine

My Plan to Enjoy My Day

Today's day and date: [M] [T] [W] [T] [F] [S] [S]　Day: [　　]　Month: [　　]　Year: [　　]

What did you enjoy most today?

Assign intensity on the scale from 1 to 20 (most intense)

>>Stress :

>>Overall Mood :

What are you grateful for today?

>>Tiredness :

>>Length of Sleeping (In hours) :

What would you like to do for yourself?
1.
2.
3.
4.

> The present moment is filled with joy and happiness. If you are attentive, you will see it.
> Thich Nhat Hanh

My rewards for what has been successfully Done or just for the enjoyment of the day

My priorities for today
1.
2.
3.
4.

What inspired you today?

Did you have 5 minutes of stillness this morning?

[ ] Yes　　[ ] No

Did you realize a tense feeling during the day and after the experience of stillness this morning

[ ] Yes　　[ ] No

[ ] Morning Routine　[ ] Evening Routine

My Plan For Fulfilling of My Life Dreams

What would I like to do?

1	
2	
3	
4	

Who is involved in my idea what to do?

1	
2	
3	
4	

What are my expectations?

1	
2	
3	
4	

Is that idea one of my life dreams?

1	☐ Yes	☐ No
2	☐ Yes	☐ No
3	☐ Yes	☐ No
4	☐ Yes	☐ No

Am I Felling Stress?

How intense is my stress on the scale from 1 to 20 (Most intense)	
Monday	
Tuesday	
Wednesday	
Thursday	
Friday	

Do I need to take a break?		
Monday	Yes	No
Tuesday	Yes	No
Wednesday	Yes	No
Thursday	Yes	No
Friday	Yes	No

If no, finishing your activity doesn't mean that you can relax, true?		
Monday	Yes	No
Tuesday	Yes	No
Wednesday	Yes	No
Thursday	Yes	No
Friday	Yes	No

Am I happy at this moment		
Monday	Yes	No
Tuesday	Yes	No
Wednesday	Yes	No
Thursday	Yes	No
Friday	Yes	No

If no, why is important to continue in my activity?		
Monday	Yes	No
Tuesday	Yes	No
Wednesday	Yes	No
Thursday	Yes	No
Friday	Yes	No

If no, do I want to be happy?		
Monday	Yes	No
Tuesday	Yes	No
Wednesday	Yes	No
Thursday	Yes	No
Friday	Yes	No

My Plan to Enjoy My Day

Today's day and date: [M] [T] [W] [T] [F] [S] [S]   Day: [   ]   Month: [   ]   Year: [   ]

What did you enjoy most today?

Assign intensity on the scale from 1 to 20 (most intense)

>>Stress :

>>Overall Mood :

What are you grateful for today?

>>Tiredness :

>>Length of Sleeping (In hours) :

What would you like to do for yourself?
1.
2.
3.
4.

The present moment is filled with joy and happiness. If you are attentive, you will see it.
— Thich Nhat Hanh

My rewards for what has been successfully Done or just for the enjoyment of the day

My priorities for today
1.
2.
3.
4.

What inspired you today?

Did you have 5 minutes of stillness this morning?

[ ] Yes   [ ] No

Did you realize a tense feeling during the day and after the experience of stillness this morning

[ ] Yes   [ ] No

[ ] Morning Routine   [ ] Evening Routine

My Plan to Enjoy My Day

Today's day and date: [M] [T] [W] [T] [F] [S] [S]   Day: [   ]   Month: [   ]   Year: [   ]

What did you enjoy most today?

Assign intensity on the scale from 1 to 20 (most intense)

>>Stress :

>>Overall Mood :

>>Tiredness :

What are you grateful for today?

>>Length of Sleeping (In hours) :

What would you like to do for yourself?
1.
2.
3.
4.

The present moment is filled with joy and happiness. If you are attentive, you will see it.
— Thich Nhat Hanh

My rewards for what has been successfully Done or just for the enjoyment of the day

My priorities for today
1.
2.
3.
4.

What inspired you today?

Did you have 5 minutes of stillness this morning?

[ ] Yes   [ ] No

Did you realize a tense feeling during the day and after the experience of stillness this morning

[ ] Yes   [ ] No

[ ] Morning Routine   [ ] Evening Routine

My Plan to Enjoy My Day

Today's day and date: [M] [T] [W] [T] [F] [S] [S]   Day: [   ]   Month: [   ]   Year: [   ]

What did you enjoy most today?

Assign intensity on the scale from 1 to 20 (most intense)

>>Stress :

>>Overall Mood :

What are you grateful for today?

>>Tiredness :

>>Length of Sleeping (In hours) :

What would you like to do for yourself?
1.
2.
3.
4.

The present moment is filled with joy and happiness. If you are attentive, you will see it.
— Thich Nhat Hanh

My rewards for what has been successfully Done or just for the enjoyment of the day

My priorities for today
1.
2.
3.
4.

What inspired you today?

Did you have 5 minutes of stillness this morning?

☐ Yes   ☐ No

Did you realize a tense feeling during the day and after the experience of stillness this morning

☐ Yes   ☐ No

☐ Morning Routine   ☐ Evening Routine

My Plan to Enjoy My Day

Today's day and date: [M] [T] [W] [T] [F] [S] [S]   Day: [   ]   Month: [   ]   Year: [   ]

What did you enjoy most today?

Assign intensity on the scale from 1 to 20 (most intense)

>>Stress :

>>Overall Mood :

What are you grateful for today?

>>Tiredness :

>>Length of Sleeping (In hours) :

What would you like to do for yourself?
1.
2.
3.
4.

The present moment is filled with joy and happiness. If you are attentive, you will see it.
— Thich Nhat Hanh

My rewards for what has been successfully Done or just for the enjoyment of the day

My priorities for today
1.
2.
3.
4.

What inspired you today?

Did you have 5 minutes of stillness this morning?

[ ] Yes   [ ] No

Did you realize a tense feeling during the day and after the experience of stillness this morning

[ ] Yes   [ ] No

[ ] Morning Routine   [ ] Evening Routine

My Plan to Enjoy My Day

Today's day and date: [M] [T] [W] [T] [F] [S] [S]   Day: [ ]   Month: [ ]   Year: [ ]

What did you enjoy most today?

Assign intensity on the scale from 1 to 20 (most intense)

>>Stress :

>>Overall Mood :

What are you grateful for today?

>>Tiredness :

>>Length of Sleeping (In hours) :

What would you like to do for yourself?
1.
2.
3.
4.

The present moment is filled with joy and happiness. If you are attentive, you will see it.
— Thich Nhat Hanh

My rewards for what has been successfully Done or just for the enjoyment of the day

My priorities for today
1.
2.
3.
4.

What inspired you today?

Did you have 5 minutes of stillness this morning?

☐ Yes   ☐ No

Did you realize a tense feeling during the day and after the experience of stillness this morning

☐ Yes   ☐ No

☐ Morning Routine   ☐ Evening Routine

My Plan to Enjoy My Day

Today's day and date: [M] [T] [W] [T] [F] [S] [S] Day: [   ] Month: [   ] Year: [   ]

What did you enjoy most today?

Assign intensity on the scale from 1 to 20 (most intense)

>>Stress :

>>Overall Mood :

>>Tiredness :

What are you grateful for today?

>>Length of Sleeping (In hours) :

What would you like to do for yourself?
1.
2.
3.
4.

The present moment is filled with joy and happiness. If you are attentive, you will see it.
— Thich Nhat Hanh

My rewards for what has been successfully Done or just for the enjoyment of the day

My priorities for today
1.
2.
3.
4.

What inspired you today?

Did you have 5 minutes of stillness this morning?

☐ Yes   ☐ No

Did you realize a tense feeling during the day and after the experience of stillness this morning

☐ Yes   ☐ No

☐ Morning Routine   ☐ Evening Routine

My Plan to Enjoy My Day

Today's day and date: [M] [T] [W] [T] [F] [S] [S]   Day: [   ]   Month: [   ]   Year: [   ]

What did you enjoy most today?

Assign intensity on the scale from 1 to 20 (most intense)

>>Stress :

>>Overall Mood :

What are you grateful for today?

>>Tiredness :

>>Length of Sleeping (In hours) :

What would you like to do for yourself?
1.
2.
3.
4.

The present moment is filled with joy and happiness. If you are attentive, you will see it.

— Thich Nhat Hanh

My rewards for what has been successfully Done or just for the enjoyment of the day

My priorities for today
1.
2.
3.
4.

What inspired you today?

Did you have 5 minutes of stillness this morning?

☐ Yes   ☐ No

Did you realize a tense feeling during the day and after the experience of stillness this morning

☐ Yes   ☐ No

☐ Morning Routine   ☐ Evening Routine

www.ingramcontent.com/pod-product-compliance
Lightning Source LLC
LaVergne TN
LVHW011728060526
838200LV00051B/3076